ICE AGE ANIMALS
CAVE BEARS

BY ELIZABETH NEUENFELDT
ILLUSTRATIONS BY MAT EDWARDS

EPIC

BELLWETHER MEDIA • MINNEAPOLIS, MN

EPIC BOOKS are no ordinary books. They burst with intense action, high-speed heroics, and shadows of the unknown. Are you ready for an Epic adventure?

This edition first published in 2025 by Bellwether Media, Inc.

No part of this publication may be reproduced in whole or in part without written permission of the publisher. For information regarding permission, write to Bellwether Media, Inc., Attention: Permissions Department, 6012 Blue Circle Drive, Minnetonka, MN 55343.

Library of Congress Cataloging-in-Publication Data

Names: Neuenfeldt, Elizabeth, author.
Title: Cave bears / by Elizabeth Neuenfeldt.
Description: Minneapolis, MN : Bellwether Media, Inc., 2025. | Series: Epic: Ice age animals | Includes bibliographical references and index. | Audience: Ages 7-12 | Audience: Grades 2-3 |
Summary: "Engaging images accompany information about cave bears. The combination of high-interest subject matter and light text is intended for students in grades 2 through 7"-- Provided by publisher.
Identifiers: LCCN 2024019765 (print) | LCCN 2024019766 (ebook) | ISBN 9798893040395 (library binding) | ISBN 9798893041583 (paperback) | ISBN 9781644879795 (ebook).
Subjects: LCSH: Cave bear–Juvenile literature. | Animals, Fossil–Juvenile literature.
Classification: LCC QE882.C15 N473 2025 (print) | LCC QE882.C15 (ebook) | DDC 569.78--dc23/eng/20240507
LC record available at https://lccn.loc.gov/2024019765
LC ebook record available at https://lccn.loc.gov/2024019766

Text copyright © 2025 by Bellwether Media, Inc. EPIC and associated logos are trademarks and/or registered trademarks of Bellwether Media, Inc. Bellwether Media is a division of Chrysalis Education Group.

Editor: Betsy Rathburn   Designer: Jeffrey Kollock

Printed in the United States of America, North Mankato, MN.

TABLE OF CONTENTS

WHAT WERE CAVE BEARS?	4
THE LIVES OF CAVE BEARS	10
FOSSILS AND EXTINCTION	16
GET TO KNOW THE CAVE BEAR	20
GLOSSARY	22
TO LEARN MORE	23
INDEX	24

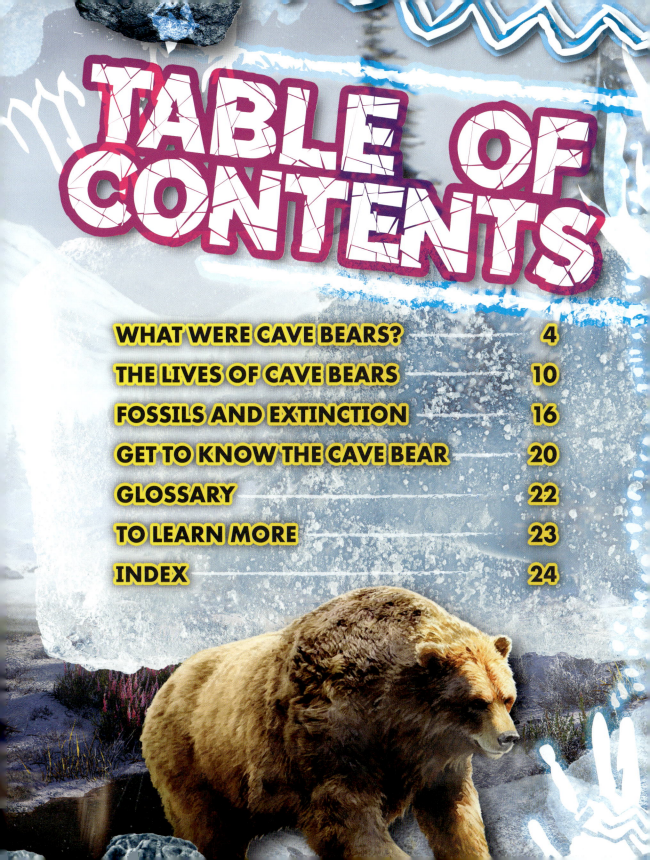

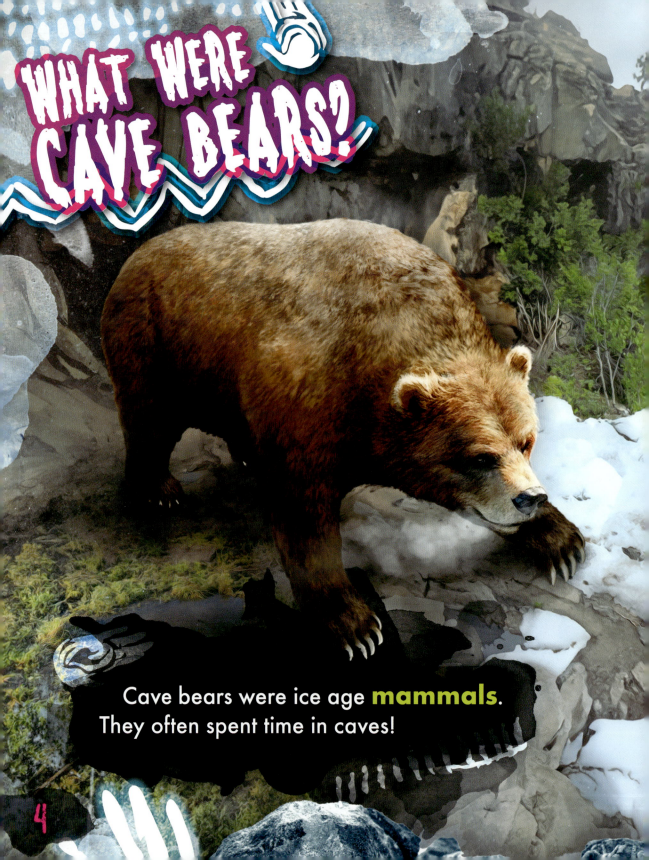

WHAT WERE CAVE BEARS?

Cave bears were ice age **mammals**. They often spent time in caves!

CAVE BEAR RANGE MAP

● = range

EARTH

WHEN
First lived during the Pleistocene epoch

These bears first appeared over 100,000 years ago. This was during the **Pleistocene epoch**. They lived in forests and mountains across Europe and Asia.

Cave bears were huge. They could weigh more than 2,000 pounds (907 kilograms). Cave bears walked on four legs. They sometimes stood on their back legs. They could stand 11.5 feet (3.5 meters) tall!

CAVE BEAR SIZE COMPARISON

11.5 feet (3.5 meters) tall on back legs

10 feet (3 meters)

5 feet (1.5 meters)

REFRIGERATORS — CAVE BEAR — HUMANS

Cave bears had two layers of fur.
They stayed warm during cold winters!

cave

LEAVING THEIR MARKS

Cave bears made claw marks on cave walls. These marks can still be seen in some caves today!

sharp claws

Cave bears stood on strong legs. They also had sharp claws on their feet. These helped cave bears climb deep into caves.

THE LIVES OF CAVE BEARS

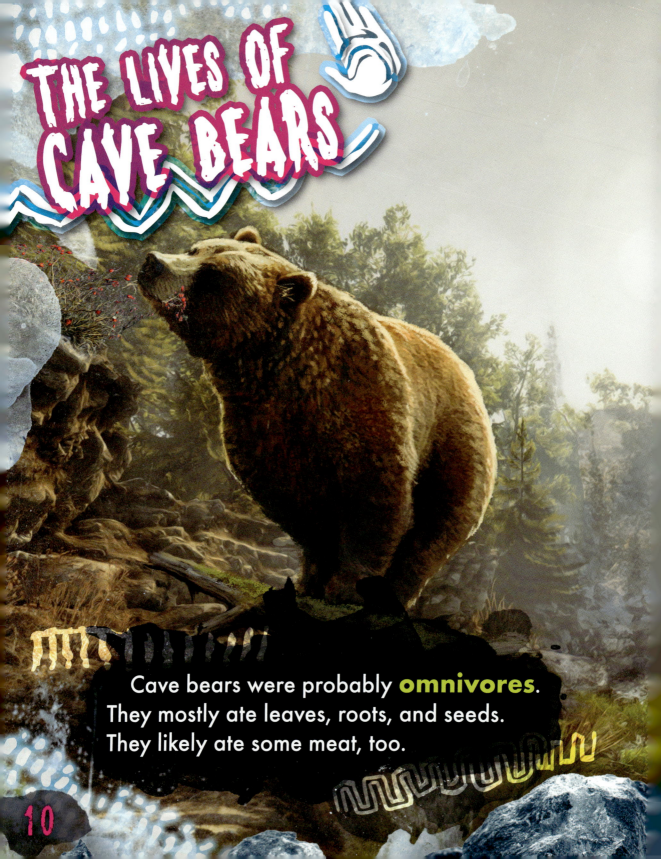

Cave bears were probably **omnivores**. They mostly ate leaves, roots, and seeds. They likely ate some meat, too.

CAVE BEAR DIET

TYPE: omnivores

roots • seeds • meat

Cave bears ate a lot during warmer months. In winter, plants became **scarce**. Cave bears **hibernated**.

Cave bears hibernated in caves. They hibernated in groups. Groups came back to the same caves to hibernate each year.

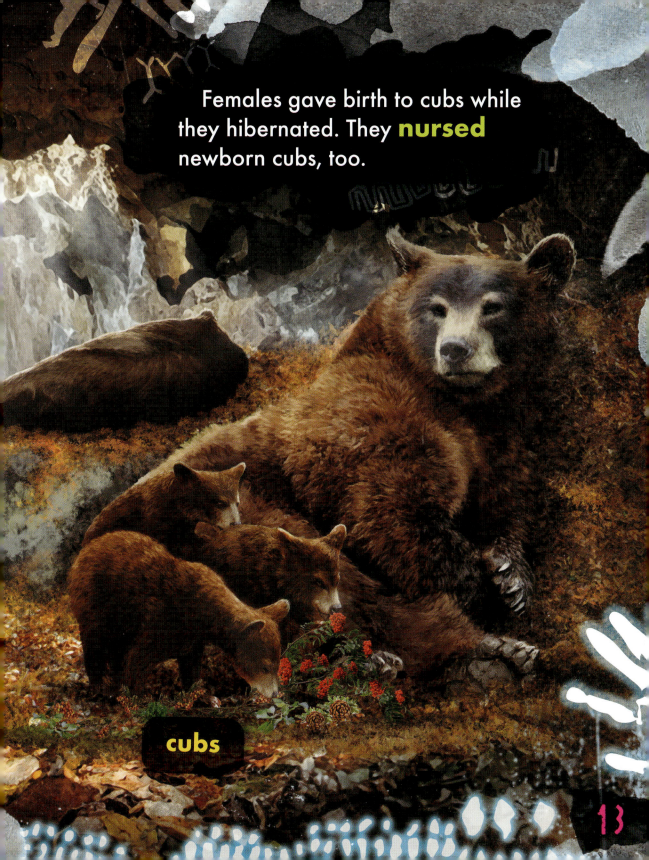

Females gave birth to cubs while they hibernated. They **nursed** newborn cubs, too.

cubs

Cave bears had few **predators**. Wolves and cave hyenas hunted sick cave bears.

Humans hunted cave bears for food and fur. They may have fought cave bears for shelter. Cave bears fought back with their sharp claws.

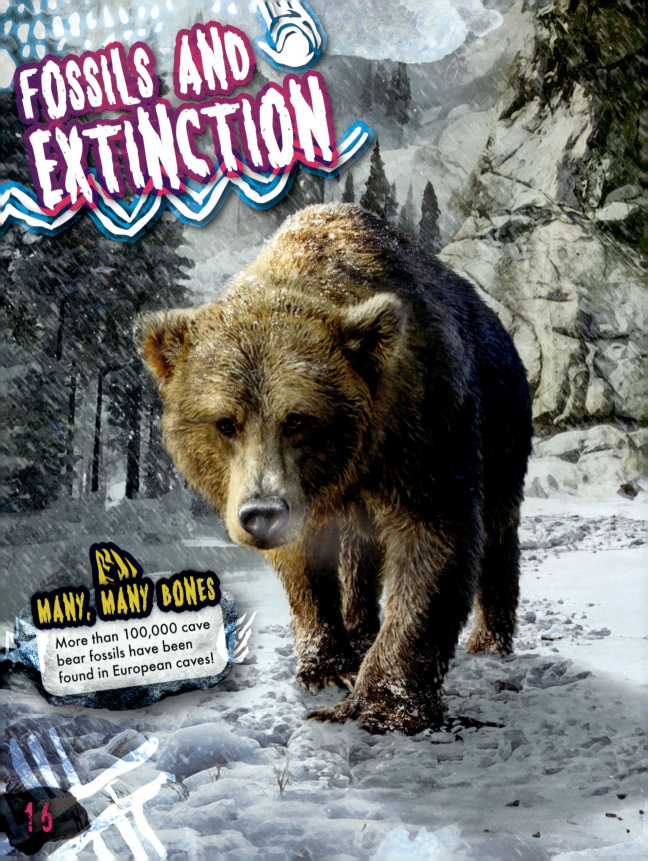

FOSSILS AND EXTINCTION

MANY, MANY BONES
More than 100,000 cave bear fossils have been found in European caves!

FAMOUS FOSSIL FIND

WHERE
Chauvet-Pont d'Arc Cave, France

WHEN
December 18, 1994

FOUND BY
Jean-Marie Chauvet, Éliette Brunel, and Christian Hillaire

FAMOUS FOR
Location of many cave bear fossils and more than 1,000 cave paintings from around 32,000 years ago

EUROPE

Cave bears went **extinct** around 24,000 years ago. This may have been caused by humans or the changing **climate**. Scientists are not sure.

Cave bear **fossils** have been found for **centuries**. Most are found in caves.

Cave bears are related to brown bears. They share **DNA**! Like cave bears, brown bears hibernate. They also have thick fur and strong claws. But cave bears were bigger.

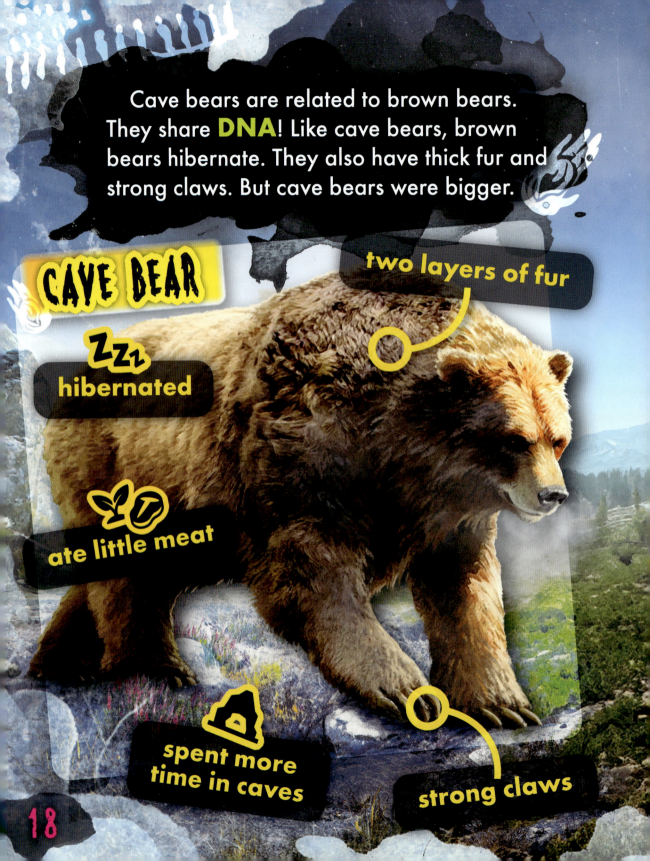

CAVE BEAR

hibernated

two layers of fur

ate little meat

spent more time in caves

strong claws

Cave bears are gone. But brown bears help us learn more about them!

BROWN BEAR

- spends less time in caves
- two layers of fur
- hibernates
- eats more meat
- strong claws

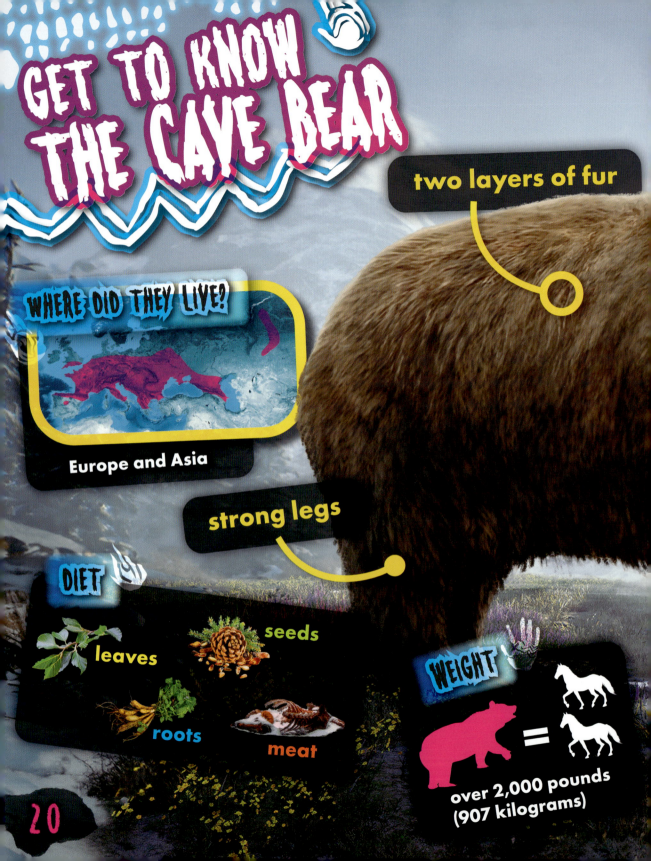

WHEN DID THEY LIVE?

160,000 to 90,000 years ago
Early modern humans first appear

over 100,000 years ago
Cave bears first appear

around 24,000 years ago
Cave bears go extinct

WHO RECORDED THE FIRST FOSSIL?

Johann Friedrich Esper in **1774**

sharp claws

HEIGHT 5.6 feet (1.7 meters) tall at the shoulders

GLOSSARY

centuries—periods of 100 years

climate—the long-term weather in a particular place

DNA—information carried in the cells of living things

extinct—no longer living

fossils—the remains of living things that lived long ago

hibernated—spent the winter in a sleeping or resting state

mammals—warm-blooded animals that have backbones and feed their young milk

nursed—gave cubs milk to drink

omnivores—animals that eat plants and animals

Pleistocene epoch—a time in history that lasted from around 2.58 million years ago to around 11,000 years ago and included the last ice age

predators—animals that hunt other animals for food

scarce—lacking in quantity or number

TO LEARN MORE

AT THE LIBRARY

Green, Sara. *Caves*. Minneapolis, Minn.: Bellwether Media, 2022.

King, SJ. *The Secret Explorers and the Ice Age Adventure*. New York, N.Y.: DK Publishing, 2022.

Riggs, Kate. *Brown Bears*. Mankato, Minn.: The Creative Company, 2023.

ON THE WEB

FACTSURFER

Factsurfer.com gives you a safe, fun way to find more information.

1. Go to www.factsurfer.com.

2. Enter "cave bears" into the search box and click 🔍.

3. Select your book cover to see a list of related content.

INDEX

Asia, 5
brown bears, 18, 19
caves, 4, 8, 9, 12, 16, 17
claws, 9, 15, 18
climate, 17
climb, 9
cubs, 13
diet, 11
DNA, 18
Europe, 5, 16
extinct, 17
famous fossil find, 17
females, 13
food, 10, 11, 15
fossils, 16, 17

fur, 8, 15, 18
get to know, 20–21
groups, 12
hibernated, 11, 12, 13, 18
humans, 15, 17
legs, 7, 9
mammals, 4
nursed, 13
omnivores, 10
Pleistocene epoch, 5
predators, 14
range map, 5
size, 7, 18
winters, 8, 11

The images in this book are reproduced through the courtesy of: Mat Edwards, front cover, pp. 4-5, 6-7, 8-9, 10-11, 12-13, 14-15, 16-17, 18-19, 20-21.